THE MILITARY EXPERIENCE.

Special Operations:

SNIPERS

THE MILITARY EXPERIENCE.

Special Operations:
SNIPERS

DON NARDO

MORGAN REYNOLDS
PUBLISHING

GREENSBORO, NORTH CAROLINA

The Military Experience.
Special Operations: Snipers
Copyright © 2013 by Morgan Reynolds Publishing

Library of Congress Cataloging-in-Publication Data

Nardo, Don, 1947-
 The military experience : special operations : snipers / by Don
Nardo.
    p. cm.
 Includes bibliographical references and index.
 ISBN 978-1-59935-368-5 -- ISBN 978-1-59935-369-2 (e-book) 1.
Snipers--United States. 2. Special forces (Military science)--United
States. 3. United States--Armed Forces--Commando troops. I. Title.
 UD333.N37 2013
 356'.162--dc23

                        2012028544

Printed in the United States of America
First Edition

Book cover and interior designed by:
Ed Morgan, navyblue design studio
Greensboro, NC

Table of Contents

A U.S. Army sniper team scans the horizon after reports of suspicious activity along the hilltops near Dur Baba, Afghanistan.

CHAPTER ONE

"I Am Everywhere and Nowhere"

U.S. Army Specialist Tommy Banks scans for enemy snipers at the Nineveh ancient ruins in Mosul, Iraq.

American sea captain Richard Phillips had no idea he was about to be at the center of a violent international incident. In the first days of April 2009 he was quietly piloting his 17,000-ton cargo ship. Called the *Maersk Alabama,* it had a crew of twenty men. The vessel entered the Indian Ocean on a routine trading mission to the African nation of Kenya.

What happened on April 8 was anything but routine, however. Four pirates suddenly boarded the ship and took Captain Phillips prisoner. Natives of another African country, Somalia, the pirates wanted to seize the ship. But the crew dutifully followed emergency procedure. Led by the ship's engineer, they entered a well-fortified "secure" room. Then they transferred the vessel's controls to that room, making it impossible for the pirates to operate the ship.

The container ship MV *Maersk Alabama* leaves Mombasa, Kenya, on April 21, 2009, after a pirate attack that took her captain hostage.

A CHANGE OF PLANS

This forced the pirates to change their plans. Taking Captain Phillips with them, they boarded an 18-foot (5.4-meter) lifeboat and headed for home. Like many Somali pirates before them, they hoped to demand a large sum of money in exchange for their hostage. But soon U.S. warships, including the USS *Bainbridge*, caught up with the lifeboat. A tense standoff ensued. The pirates, who had machine guns, said they would kill Phillips if the Americans tried to capture them.

The stressful situation went on for three days. During that time one of the pirates surrendered so that he could get medical treatment for a wound he had suffered while kidnapping Phillips. That left three pirates in the lifeboat with their American prisoner. Also, the captain of the *Bainbridge* tried to negotiate with the pirates. However, these talks rapidly broke down.

THE MILITARY EXPERIENCE.

The guided-missile destroyer USS *Bainbridge* (DDG 96) tows the lifeboat from the *Maersk Alabama* to the amphibious assault ship USS *Boxer* (LHD 4), in the background, to be processed for evidence after the successful rescue of Captain Richard Phillips.

Meanwhile, behind the scenes U.S. officials hatched a daring rescue plan. President Barack Obama ordered a unit of American commandos to hurry to the scene of the standoff. These men were members of the elite Navy SEALs. Moreover, they were specially trained as snipers, expert marksmen able to make seemingly impossible shots at great distances. Their orders were clear. Obama told them that if Phillips's life was at any point in looming danger, they should target the pirates and shoot to kill.

This was exactly what occurred, as told by *New York Times* reporter Robert D. McFadden. At dusk on April 12, he wrote, three SEAL snipers:

> fixed night-vision scopes to their high-powered rifles, getting ready for action. What they saw was the head and shoulders of two of the pirates emerging from the rear hatch of the lifeboat. Through the window of the front hatch they saw the third pirate, pointing his [gun] at the back of Captain Phillips. . . . Each [sniper] took a target and fired one shot.

Two minutes later, armed sailors from the *Bainbridge* entered the lifeboat. They found the three pirates sprawled dead. Each had a gaping hole in his head. Captain Phillips was safe and soon that fact inspired joyful cheers from the crews of the nearby ships.

A DEADLY, VALUABLE WEAPON

The exact locations the SEALs were in when they shot the pirates remain a secret to this day. The very identities of these commandos are also uncertain. In part, this is to protect them. As a Navy spokesman explained, the SEALs and members of other U.S. special ops groups "work in the most sensitive areas and on the most important missions. If their identities were made public it could jeopardize their safety, or that of the missions they are on."

Keeping the shooters in the shadows is also the way that military snipers prefer to work. "I am everywhere and nowhere," said former U.S. Army Ranger sniper Joe LeBleu. "I exist to not exist. I am the shadow my enemies fear. I am a well-tuned precision instrument that can change the direction of a war with one shot." What he meant was that one shot by a sniper can remove an enemy leader from the picture. That might have serious negative consequences for enemy forces in general.

Yet skilled snipers are capable of much more. In fact, an increased use of snipers by the U.S. military is steadily changing the nature of modern warfare. As former Navy SEAL sniper Brandon Webb pointed out:

> Something fundamental has changed in the way we wage war and keep the peace. In the wars of our fathers and their fathers, the decisive victories were won by tank battalions and overwhelming air support. In today's world of suicide bombers . . . terrorism [and] piracy, the fortunes and well-being of nations rest increasingly in the hands, reflexes, and capabilities of individual warriors like [U.S. military snipers].

For example, snipers have made a major difference in the long war in Afghanistan. Before a large unit of U.S. Marine snipers went there in 2011, enemy forces attacked Americans almost every time they left a local U.S. base. Soon, however, the newly arrived snipers, always remaining unseen, began picking off enemy soldiers one by one. That sent a wave of fear through the opposing forces. And that made them more likely to try negotiating. In this and other ways, snipers are proving to be among the most deadly and valuable weapons in the U.S. military arsenal.

U.S. Marine Corps Corporal Scott P. Ruggio fires his MK-11 sniper rifle in the first stage of a three-day platoon competition in Djibouti in East Africa.

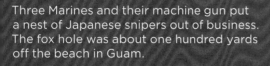

Three Centuries of U.S. Snipers

Snipers have taken part in all of America's wars, beginning in the
late 1700s. Up until recent times, they were most often used to
kill enemy officers from a distance. The battle of Saratoga, in the
American Revolution in September 1777, was a well-known example. U.S. marksmen repeatedly targeted and killed British officers.
This helped to secure the American victory. However, U.S. snipers
long remained little more than soldiers who happened to be un-
usually good shots. Sniper training was limited in scope. And these
fighters knew little about the art of concealment. Only during the
late twentieth century did the U.S. military start training snipers to
be elite, highly trained commandos.

fact BOX

Chris Kyle Shatters the Record

With a record of 255 kills, American Navy SEAL Chris Kyle easily surpassed the long-held U.S. record of 109 kills set by Army sniper Adelbert F. Waldron during the Vietnam War.

Accuracy International
G22 Arctic 7.62mm
Sniper Rifle

U.S. Navy Master-At-Arms 2nd Class Kevin Dennis plays the role of sniper during air base defense training maneuvers at Misawa Air Force Base in Japan.

CHAPTER TWO

Trained to OPERATE Independently

All branches of the U.S. military have their own small units of snipers. Most of them are commandos, also known as special ops fighters. "Special ops" is short for "special operations forces," or SOF. Among others, they include the Air Force's "Pararescue Jumpers," or PJs; the Navy's SEALs and Special Boat Crewmen; and the Army's Delta Force, Green Berets, and Rangers. Members of such special ops units are elite warriors who carry out missions that are too difficult for average soldiers and sailors.

Most U.S. military snipers first train to become commandos. That makes them top-quality, fearsome fighters. Then they go to sniper school, where they develop even more specialized skills. When they graduate, these tough, awesome marksmen are among the finest fighters in the world.

The United States military has several excellent sniper schools. Not long ago, legendary SEAL sniper and sniper instructor Brandon Webb was asked to rate them. In his opinion, all are worthwhile. But some, he said, stand out as exceptional. One is the Army's SOTIC, which stands for Special Ops Target Interdiction Course. It is held at the Army's facilities in Fort Bragg, North Carolina. Webb also singled out the sniper school at the Naval Surface Warfare Center near Indianapolis, Indiana.

fact BOX

The Marine Sniper Program

Among the finest of the U.S. military sniper training programs, according to former SEAL sniper Brandon Webb, is that of the U.S. Marine Corps. Versions of it exist at Marine bases in Virginia, North Carolina, California, and Hawaii.

Sergeant Joshua Heidecker peers through the scope mounted on his M40-A3 sniper rifle.

Sergeant Nicholas Irving takes aim during the "Defensive Shoot" event at Wagner Range in Fort Benning, Georgia, during the ninth annual U.S. Army International Sniper Competition.

U.S. Army Specialist Nicholas Ranstad (*right*), a sniper, leads a fire team of Air Force joint terminal air controllers in search of a high-value target during an exercise in support of Allied Strike II at U.S. Army Garrison Hohenfels in Germany.

THE PRIMARY MISSION

Whichever sniper school a recruit attends, he is in for long weeks of extremely difficult training. Contrary to popular notions, the trainees do not spend most of their time lying or sitting around practicing long-distance shots. These schools teach a great deal more, as explained by former Air Force weapons expert Rod Powers:

> A lot of people have the misconception that to be a good sniper, you [only] have to be a good shooter. Shooting is only 20 percent of the course at the Army Sniper School. It takes a patient person, a disciplined person, a person who is used to working alone. In addition to marksmanship skills, the school instructs on detecting and stalking a target, and estimating the range of a target. The course also covers concealment and camouflage, as well as observation exercises.

By "observation," Powers means the art of reconnaissance, or "special recon." It consists of gathering as much information, or "intelligence," about the enemy as possible. Indeed, one expert observer points out that "the sniper's primary mission" often has little to do with simply "pulling a trigger." Rather:

> The main battlefield role of the sniper is reconnaissance. Because snipers are masters of stealth [secrecy], they are perfectly suited to sneak behind enemy lines to provide [U.S. commanders] with information about the enemy's size, strength, and location.

THE POWER OF LIFE AND DEATH

To be effective, snipers must also be in top physical condition. And the training they receive in sniper school strongly emphasizes vigorous exercise. This includes doing lots of push-ups, sit-ups, and long distance runs. In short, it is roughly the same physical training given to recruits for the Army Rangers and Navy SEALs.

However, more than anything else the sniper schools try to turn out independent warriors. These are individuals who can work on their own and be trusted to make the right choices. "Commanders aren't looking for 'good shots' or 'natural born killers,'" military observer Robert Valdes says. What they *are* looking for "is a soldier that possesses good decision making and a level head." An unnamed former Ranger sniper agrees and adds:

> You don't want a real hot head to be a sniper. Snipers need to be able to work on their own. . . . So when you're not with your unit you need to be able to make sound decisions on your own without having to [ask your superiors], "What should I do here?"

To achieve this level of independence, during training each recruit spends a fair amount of time on his own. Some of it involves stalking. This consists of sneaking through a wilderness area undetected by the instructors—an extremely difficult task. All of the training is equally hard and for two good reasons. First, the graduated snipers will hold the power of life and death in their hands. Second, as Joe LeBleu points out, the training determines "who will quit when things get tough. Someone who quits in training will certainly quit in combat, and could end up getting you killed."

Compensating for Wind

There are many important calculations an expert marksman must do to make a successful long-distance shot. One of the chief ones is estimating wind speed. This is because the faster the wind is moving, the more it can push a bullet off-course. Thus, the sniper must compensate, or make up for, the effect of wind. He does this by aiming slightly off the center of his target. Once he has fired, the wind pushes the bullet back toward that central point. In training, the recruits start out figuring wind speed by observing flags. Next, they learn to judge it by looking at the way the wind blows things like smoke, leaves, and dust. Still another way to do it is the "spotting scope method." Former SEAL sniper Howard Wasdin explains:

> When the sun heats the earth, the air near the surface ripples in waves. The wind causes these waves to move in its direction. To see the waves, the sniper focuses on an object near the target. Rotating the eyepiece a quarter turn . . . he focuses on the area in front of the target area, which makes the heat waves become visible. Slow wind causes big waves, while fast wind flattens them out.

An aerial precision marksman with the Pacific Tactical Law Enforcement Team, home based at Marine Corps Recruit Depot San Diego, prepares to engage a target in a required training exercise on his Barrett .50 caliber sniper rifle.

CHAPTER THREE

A Sniper's WEAPONS and GEAR

U.S. Marine Corps Corporal Joe Rattlif peers through the scope mounted to a Barrett Light Fifty Model 82A1 sniping rifle while training at the Military Operations in Urban Terrain facility at Camp Pendleton in California.

All U.S. commandos rely heavily on their weapons and the other equipment they carry while on missions. This is only natural. After all, a special ops fighter must be able to defend himself against enemy attacks. He must also be able to survive in the often harsh settings in which he finds himself. In any number of situations, therefore, his weapons and gear can make the difference between life and death.

The connection between a commando and his primary weapon is well illustrated by the case of the sniper. "A sniper's relationship with his weapon is very special," former Marine sniper Milo S. Afong remarked. "He is the ultimate caretaker of his rifle. And in return the weapon keeps him alive. A sniper has to give constant attention to his rifle, as if it were a baby. He cleans it, dresses it, [and] protects it from the elements. [He] never loses it and always guards it with his life."

Indeed, only one situation demands that a sniper part with his trusty rifle. It is when he knows he is about to die or be captured. In that case, he is trained either to dispose of the weapon or to permanently disable it. That way the enemy cannot use it against other American fighters. "Whatever you do," Afong said, "do not let the enemy have control of your rifle!"

A RANGE OF DIFFERENT GUNS

As for which rifle a sniper uses, he has several good ones to choose from. Yet most snipers do not use a single kind of gun all the time. Former SEAL Chris Kyle, often called "the most lethal sniper in U.S. military history," explained. "In the field," he said, "I matched the weapon to the job and the situation." He learned how to use a range of different guns, so he was "prepared not only to use them all, but also to choose the right one for the job."

The "right one" can sometimes be the M24. In fact, it is the most common sniper rifle used by members of the U.S. special forces community. Joe LeBleu calls it the "standard issue to all U.S. Army snipers." A recently upgraded version of the M24 is fairly accurate for targets up to 1,400 yards (1281 meters) away. Another sniper rifle, the M40A3, is similar in many ways to the M24. The M40A3 is standard issue to most U.S. Marine snipers.

U.S. Army Specialist Chantha Bun (*foreground*), armed with an M24 sniper rifle and an AN/PVS-10 Day+Night Vision Sniper Scope, and Sergeant Anthony Davis (*background*), armed with an Accuracy Engineering tactical sniper rifle, scan for enemy activity at 4 West, an Iraqi police station located in Mosul, Iraq, following an attack by insurgents.

Both of these weapons may soon be replaced by a slightly more advanced rifle—the M110. It has an effective range of about 3,280 feet (1,000 meters), or well more than half a mile. Also, when fully loaded, it weighs 15 pounds (6.8 kg). It was first used in combat in Afghanistan in 2007, and most of the soldiers who used it gave it high marks.

Much bigger and heavier is the M82A3 50-caliber sniper rifle. One former U.S. sniper described it as being "capable of penetrating armor and other tough obstacles like car doors, windows," and even the walls of houses. "This weapon can reach out to 1,800 meters (more than 18 football fields)." The M82's main drawback is its weight. "Fully loaded with a ten-round magazine [the container holding the bullets], the rifle weighs in at 32.5 pounds [14.7 kg]." That makes it too heavy to lug around for very long if the shooter is both on foot and on the move.

fact BOX

Costs of Sniper Rifles

Sniper rifles, especially when equipped with special scopes and other equipment, are precision instruments. Not surprisingly, that makes them very expensive. The average sniper rifle costs between $8,000 and $15,000.

Marine Corps Corporal Dustin Hill, a scout sniper team leader, fires a round downrange from an M82A3 50-caliber special application scoped rifle.

SCOPES AND OTHER GEAR

Another item that makes a sniper's rifle "fully loaded" is perhaps the most important piece of gear he carries, his scope. That term is short for "telescope." And snipers' scopes are just that—small telescopes mounted on the tops of their rifles. In his popular book, *American Sniper,* Chris Kyle explained how a sniper chooses the right scope:

> Overseas, I used a 32-power scope. The powers on a scope refer to the magnification. . . . Without getting too technical, the higher the power, the better a shooter can see at a distance. But there are tradeoffs, depending on the situation and the scope. Scopes should be chosen with a mind toward the situation they'll be used in.

Also depending on the situation, military snipers carry a fair amount of other gear. Afong claimed that on an average mission he carried "two radios, night vision [goggles], global positioning devices [GPS], flares, [and] a laser range finder, as well as ammunition and explosives." Sometimes, he said, he also carried one or two cameras and a laptop computer. Clearly, to be effective a sniper must think ahead and make sure he is prepared for a wide range of possible situations.

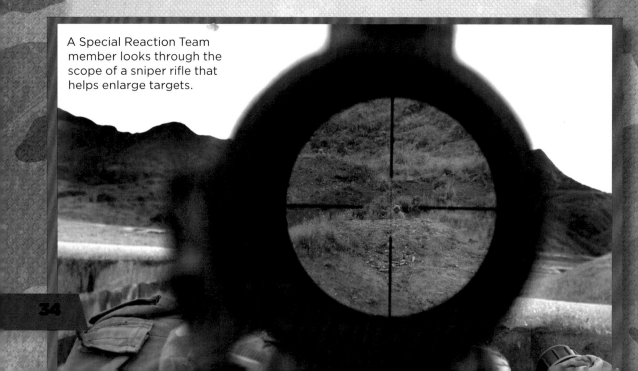

A Special Reaction Team member looks through the scope of a sniper rifle that helps enlarge targets.

The Lives He SAVED

One thing that people frequently ask retired snipers is how they felt about killing other human beings. Or how did they *justify* taking others' lives?

Former U.S. Marine Corps sniper Carlos Hathcock answered: "I like shooting . . . but I never did enjoy killing anybody. It's my job. If I don't get those [bad guys], then they're gonna kill a lot of these kids dressed up like [U.S.] Marines." In a separate interview, Hathcock emphasized the idea that killing the enemy was a way to save American lives. "If there was a meaningful thing about [the] numbers" of people he killed, he said, "it would have been the number of lives I saved. Not the number I took."

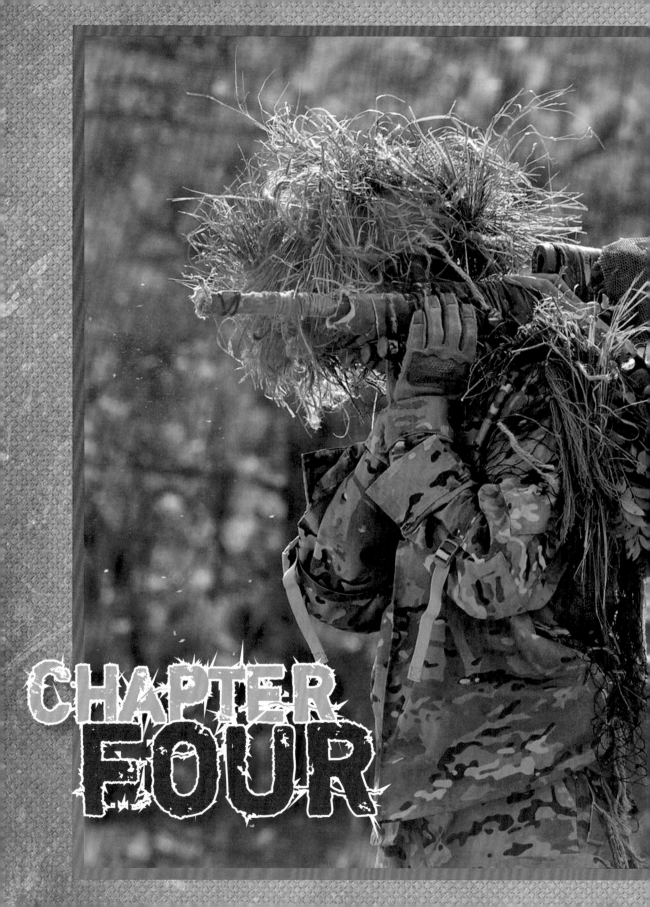

CHAPTER FOUR

Two U.S. Army snipers wearing camouflage gear known as "ghillie" suits combine to form an over-the-shoulder firing position during competitive shooting at the tenth annual International Sniper Competition in Fort Benning, Georgia.

MASTERS
of the
Tactics
of
STEALTH

U.S. Army soldiers provide
security in Masamute Valley
as they cordon and search the
village of Bala in Laghman
province, Afghanistan.

The U.S. commandos and other specially trained warriors who undergo sniper training follow routine methods in their work. These techniques or approaches are called tactics. If one could sum up a sniper's tactics in one word, it would be *secrecy*. Indeed, American military snipers are true masters of secrecy, also called stealth.

THE TWO MAIN TASKS

The importance of stealth in the sniper's profession can be plainly seen in all aspects of his missions. In his book about his experiences, former SEAL sniper Howard Wasdin described one of his instructors in sniper school. The man was one of the finest marksmen in the entire U.S. military. He told Wasdin and the other recruits about a sniper's two main jobs. One, he said, "is to support combat operations by delivering precision fire on selected targets from concealed positions."

In other words, one of a sniper's tasks is to find a good hiding place. From there, he shoots and kills one or more enemy fighters. The instructor's use of the word *selected* was crucial. "The sniper doesn't just go out there shooting any target," he explained. "He takes out the targets that will help win the battle." Those targets are usually chosen by the sniper's superior officers.

The instructor added that the sniper's other main task "is observation—gathering information." It takes up much, if not most, of the sniper's time on a given mission. The manner in which these fighters gather intelligence about the enemy depends on the situation. Some snipers write it down by hand. Others record it on a small laptop or other electronic device. If a sniper loses his equipment, he must commit as much information as possible to memory. Fortunately, snipers are trained to be observant and detail-oriented.

STAYING HIDDEN

Wasdin and other former snipers emphasize that when possible a sniper does these jobs with the aid of a comrade. That second person is called a spotter. The two work as a team. They help each other to survive in the wild and hopefully to make the mission a success.

The first thing the team members do is find a suitable hiding place. To make sure the enemy cannot see them, they often employ camouflage. It consists of objects, patterns, and/or colors that make them and their gear blend in with their surroundings. Sometimes they build a hide, a small, makeshift structure made of branches or other natural materials.

They may also use a ghillie suit, a special outfit that also takes advantage of the concept of camouflage. Usually such a suit begins with an old military uniform. The wearer dyes it, giving it colors that match the setting he will be working in. He also sews on netting in various places. To that he attaches shredded cloth, along with leaves, twigs, and other natural materials. In addition to camouflaging his body, he might also make a smaller ghillie suit for his rifle. That way an enemy scout won't spot the gun's barrel, revealing the sniper's location.

A Marine sniper wearing a ghillie suit advances through a forest during a training exercise.

fact BOX

A Ghillie in the Grass

The term *ghillie* is Scottish for an old-fashioned kind of game warden who worked on wealthy estates. When he wanted to capture a deer or other animal alive, he laid very still in tall grass. As the creature ambled by, the ghillie leapt out and grabbed it.

TAKING THE SHOT

Once satisfied that they are well hidden, the sniper and spotter prepare to take the shot (or shots). The first step is to use a scope to pinpoint the target. One expert observer writes:

> The spotter carries his own special scope that is much more powerful than the scope on a sniper rifle. The spotter uses his scope to help the sniper observe [the target] and set up the shot. The two soldiers work together to get to the [target] safely and discreetly and then set up a [firing] position.

A sniper's firing position is the specific way he arranges his body to make a shot. One of the more common positions is called "prone supported." In it, the sniper lies prone, or on his belly, with his legs spread shoulder width. His rifle rests mostly in front of him, with the barrel supported by a small wooden or metal stand. Such a stand, called a bipod, is often attached to the barrel's underside and unfolds when needed. (Some bipods come as separate attachments.) A sniper can also use his rucksack (backpack) or some other object to support the barrel.

There are, in addition, a number of kneeling and standing positions. In each, the rifle barrel can be supported or unsupported. Sometimes the spotter offers his opinion about which position will work best in a given situation. But the sniper, who is the team's senior member, has the final say.

After the sniper fires, the spotter carefully watches the bullet's path and the results of the shot. In the unlikely event that the bullet misses the target, the spotter helps the sniper prepare for a second shot. Usually the first shot is successful, however. And often the two men spend the rest of the mission gathering intelligence. In that case, Robert Valdes, explains, they typically "take turns using the spotter scope to spy on the enemy. This helps to avoid eye fatigue and allows one team member to rest while the other watches."

Finally, the sniper and spotter leave the target area as quietly as they entered it. It is common for a helicopter to pick them up at a preplanned spot. The chopper then ferries them back to their home base. There, they hand over whatever information they have gathered. Frequently, they can take pride in having made a major contribution to the larger war effort.

Sniper and Boatswain Mate Third Class Todd Hubert is assisted by his spotter, Seaman Chad Luck, who calls wind direction and determines where the rounds impact through the spotting scope.

CHAPTER FIVE

U.S. Military
SNIPERS
in ACTION

U.S. Army Private First Class Joshua Clark and Specialist Saikan Corbitt move behind mud walls in order to take over an enemy sniper position in the Charkh District in Logar province, Afghanistan.

Some of the most memorable and thrilling feats performed by military heroes in the past two centuries have been those of snipers. These exploits were accomplished by legendary individuals from many parts of the world. Germany, Russia, Canada, Finland, Ireland, and several other nations contributed to the ranks of the greatest snipers.

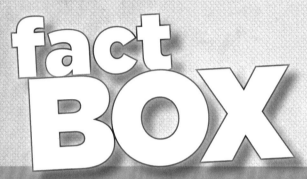

fact BOX

Thomas Plunkett

Perhaps the most famous Irish sniper was Thomas Plunkett. In 1809, he shot and killed a French general at a distance of 1,968 feet (600 meters). Mechanically speaking, rifles were not very accurate back then. So this was viewed as an incredible piece of marksmanship.

A number of Americans were also among the finest snipers in history. During the early 1800s, numerous men who lived in the U.S. western frontier had to hunt to feed their families. And some of them became crack shots. Hundreds of such skilled hunters fought for both sides in the American Civil War (1861-1865). Some of them made impressive long-distance shots in that conflict. A young Confederate soldier known only as "Sergeant Grace" was one of them.

On May 9, 1864, at the start of the Battle of Spotsylvania, he killed Union General John Sedgwick at a distance of 3,000 feet (915 meters).

The twentieth century and early years of the twenty-first witnessed the exploits of more legendary U.S. military snipers. During those years the quality of rifles and scopes improved considerably. In addition, the Army, Marines, and other military branches developed the excellent sniper schools that continue to turn out top-notch marksmen today. Those years also witnessed many highly patriotic young men volunteering to train as snipers. The combination of these diverse factors produced a steady stream of snipers with uncommon skill and courage.

Union General John Sedgwick

A LEGENDARY TEAM

Those personal qualities were demonstrated repeatedly during the Vietnam War, which raged in the 1960s and early 1970s. Hundreds of thousands of American soldiers went to Vietnam, in southeast Asia. They hoped to keep Communism from spreading throughout the region.

Meanwhile, the Vietnamese were sharply divided. Those in the south helped the Americans. But those in the north viewed the Americans as invaders. Their soldiers, called the Viet Cong, were tough and brave. Moreover, they knew how to blend into the jungle settings in which much of the fighting took place.

An infantry patrol moves up to assault the last Viet Cong position in Dak To, Vietnam, after an attempted overrun of the artillery position by the Viet Cong during Operation Hawthorne in 1966.

U.S. snipers did their best to counter the deadly Viet Cong fighters. Among those American marksmen were two Marines who formed what is now remembered as a legendary team. One was Carlos Hathcock, one of the finest U.S. marksmen of all time. He single-handedly trained more than six hundred men to be first-rate snipers. Among those recruits was John Burke. Hathcock and Burke became friends and often partnered together as snipers.

On one particular occasion, their mission was to hunt down small groups of Viet Cong. These enemy soldiers had been ambushing American Marines in a region dominated by steep sandy hills covered with tall grass. Hathcock and Burke found a good hiding place atop one of the hills and waited.

Marine Corps Corporal Atchley guards a Viet Cong member as he moves toward the collection point.

A U.S. Navy SEAL in Vietnam keeps his Stoner 63A light machine gun at the ready while the rest of his squad prepares demolition charges on a Viet Cong bunker.

"OUR SHOOTING GALLERY"

Soon a group of four Viet Cong appeared in the distance. As the two Americans watched them through their scopes, three more enemy soldiers came into view. Hathcock could tell by their body language that the seven men were taking a rest. "They mean to sit here a bit," he whispered to Burke, "right in the back of our shooting gallery." Burke smiled and nodded. Hathcock then told him, "You shoot the one standing guard up front. He's the closest shot. And I'll take the guard in the rear. Then start working on their circle from the right and I will from the left."

Having devised a plan of action, the two Americans opened fire almost at the same instant. By the time the sound of the shots reached the enemy soldiers, the first two of their number were dead. The other Viet Cong apparently thought that U.S. troops were attacking their flank, or side. So they mistakenly and recklessly ran straight toward the American snipers. "Hold 'em and squeeze 'em," Hathcock calmly ordered and he and Burke fired again. In the space of the next five or six seconds, they sent bullets hurtling through the bodies of all five fleeing men. "Seven rounds, seven dead Viet Cong," Hathcock said softly. Burke knew what he meant—that not a single bullet had been wasted.

THE WAVE OF THE FUTURE?

Hathcock's and Burke's swift, efficient execution of the seven enemy fighters was only one of their many successful missions. More importantly, their actions foretold how snipers would be used in later conflicts. Increasingly, they came to stalk and eliminate opposing fighters one by one. And that made the enemy worry for their own safety.

A recent example was the way U.S. snipers came to instill fear in enemy ranks in Afghanistan. As Brandon Webb said, "the 21st Century sniper is an intelligent and mature shooter." He uses "technology to increase accuracy and devastate" the enemy's sense of well-being. In Afghanistan, "bad guys" who were "up to no good" started to see "their friends disappearing." And that made the enemy less inclined to go on fighting.

It is therefore certain, Webb and other experts say, that snipers will be a vital facet of the military wave of the future. They will not completely replace tanks, ships, and planes, of course. But it is likely that well-trained and well-placed snipers will help reduce the need for large armies. As Hathcock himself shrewdly observed, "There's nothing on the battlefield more deadly than one well-aimed shot."

Gunnery Sergeant Carlos Hathcock is presented with the Silver Star during a ceremony at the Weapons Training Battalion in Quantico, Virginia.

fact BOX

A Bounty On His Head

The great American sniper Carlos Hathcock had nintey-three confirmed kills and an estimated three hundred unconfirmed ones. He was so feared by the Viet Cong that they put a $30,000 bounty on his head and sent out entire units of soldiers to find and kill him. They failed every time.

Staff Sergeants Alexander Erb (*foreground*) and Brian Little practice their sniper skills during a training scenario.

Source Notes

Chapter 1: "I Am Everywhere and Nowhere"

p. 13,   "fixed night-vision scopes . . ." Robert D. McFadden and Scott Shane, "In Rescue of Captain, Navy Kills 3 Pirates," *New York Times*, April 12, 2009.

p. 14,   "work in the most sensitive areas . . ." Navy Handbook, "SEAL Team Six Q&A," May 3, 2011, http://navyhandbook.org/262/seal-team-six-qa/.

p. 14,   "I am everywhere and nowhere . . ." Joe LeBleu, *Long Rifle: A Sniper's Story in Iraq and Afghanistan* (Guilford, CTL Lyons Press, 2009),1.

p. 14,   "Something fundamental has changed . . ." Brandon Webb, *The Red Circle: My Life in the Navy SEAL Sniper Corps and How I Trained America's Deadliest Marksmen* (New York: St. Martins, 2012), 7.

Chapter 2: Trained to Operate Independently

p. 25,   "A lot of people have . . ." Rod Powers, "Army Sniper School," http://usmilitary.about.com/od/armytrng/a/sniperschool.htm.

p. 25,   "the sniper's primary mission . . ." Robert Valdes, "How Military Snipers Work: What Does a Sniper Really Do?," http://science.howstuffworks.com/sniper1.htm.

p. 26,   "Commanders aren't looking for . . ." Robert Valdes, "How Military Snipers Work: Sniper School," http://science.howstuffworks.com/sniper8.htm.

p. 26,   "You don't want . . ." Ibid.

p. 26,   "who will quit . . ." LeBleu, *Long Rifle*,12.

p. 27,   "When the sun heats the earth . . ." Howard E. Wasdin and Stephen Templin, *SEAL Team Six: Memoirs of an Elite Navy SEAL Sniper* (New York: Thorndike, 2011), 260-261.

Chapter 3: A Sniper's Weapons and Gear

p. 30,   "A sniper's relationship . . ." Milo S. Afong, *Hogs in the Shadows: Combat Stories from Marine Snipers in Iraq* (New York: Berkley Caliber, 2007), 6.

p. 30,   "Whatever you do . . ." Ibid., 11.

p. 30,   "the most lethal sniper . . ." Chris Kyle et. al., *American Sniper: The Autobiography of the Most Lethal Sniper in U.S. Military History* (New York: William Morrow, 2012), cover.

p. 30,   "In the field . . ." Ibid.,132.

p. 31,   "standard issue to all . . ." LeBleu, *Long Rifle,* 207.

p. 32,   "capable of penetrating armor . . ." Afong, *Hogs in the Shadows,* 7.

p. 34,   "Overseas, I used . . ." Kyle et al, *American Sniper,* 138-139.

p. 34,   "two radios, night vision . . ." Afong, *Hogs in the Shadows,* 7.

p. 35,   "I like shooting . . ." Wasdin and Templin, *SEAL Team Six,*19.

p. 35,   "If there was . . ." Charles Henderson, *Silent Warrior: The Marine Sniper's Vietnam Story Continues* (New York: Berkley Books, 2000), 3.

Chapter 4: Masters of the Tactics of Stealth

p. 39,   "is to support combat operations . . ." Wasdin and Templin, *SEAL Team Six,* 259.

p. 39,   "The sniper doesn't just go . . ." Ibid., 259.

p. 39,   "is observation . . ." Ibid.

p. 42,   "The spotter carries . . ." Robert Valdes, "How Military Snipers Work: Sniper Teams," http://science.howstuffworks.com/sniper2.htm.

p. 43,   "take turns using the spotter scope . . ." Robert Valdes, "How Military Snipers Work: The Spotter," http://science.howstuffworks.com/sniper3.htm.

Chapter 5: U.S. Military Snipers in Action

p. 53,   "They mean to sit here . . ." Henderson, *Silent Warrior,* 85.

p. 54,   "Hold 'em and squeeze 'em . . ." Ibid.

p. 54,   "Seven rounds . . ." Ibid. 86.

p. 54,   "the 21st Century sniper . . ." Buck Sexton, "Are U.S. Snipers a Modern Battlefield Game Changer?," TheBlaze.com., May 10, 2012, http://www.theblaze.com/stories/are-u-s-snipers-a-modern-battlefield-game-changer-former-seal-brandon-webb-weighs-in/.

p. 54,   "There's nothing on the battlefield . . ." Henderson, *Silent Warrior,* 86.

Glossary

bipod: A small, foldable stand on which a sniper sometimes rests his rifle barrel.

camouflage: Patterns and colors designed to make military uniforms, gear, and weapons blend in with a given natural setting.

chopper: A common nickname for a helicopter.

civilian: A person who is not in the armed forces.

commando: An elite, specially trained soldier who is assigned to difficult, dangerous missions.

GPS (Global Positioning System): A network of orbiting satellites that allow people to quickly compute their exact position on Earth's surface.

ghillie suit: A homemade outfit used by a sniper to camouflage himself and stay hidden from the enemy.

hide: A makeshift shelter constructed in the woods or another wilderness area.

hostage: A person who is held somewhere against his or her will.

intelligence: Information about one's enemies.

jeopardize: To endanger.

magazine (or clip): A small container inside a gun that holds the bullets.

reconnaissance (or recon for short): Scouting, investigating, and/or information-gathering.

recruit: A soldier, sailor, or other fighter who is in training.

round: A bullet or other projectile fired from a gun.

shrewd: Wise or clever.

special ops: Short for Special Operations Forces, consisting of the U.S. Military's elite units of soldiers.

spotter: A sniper's partner, who helps him to both survive and line up shots.

stealth: Secrecy; a person who is stealthy is efficient at sneaking around and hiding.

tactics: Methods of or approaches to accomplishing a job or mission.

Bibliography

Afong, Milo S. *Hogs in the Shadows: Combat Stories from Marine Snipers in Iraq.* New York: Berkley Caliber, 2007.

Baglole, Joel. "The M110 Sniper Rifle—Weapon of Choice." http://usmilitary.about.com/od/armyweapons/a/m110.htm.

Bedard, Paul. "Top 5 Weapons of Pentagon's Deadliest Sniper." November 28, 2011, http://www.usnews.com/news/washington-whispers/articles/2011/11/28/top-5-weapons-of-pentagons-deadliest-sniper-.

CNN. "How U.S. Forces Killed Osama bin Laden." May 2, 2011, http://articles.cnn.com/2011-05-02/world/bin.laden.raid_1_bin-compound-terrorist-attacks?_s=PM:WORLD.

Cooke, Tim. *U.S. Army Special Forces.* New York: Powerkids Press, 2012.

Couch, Dick. *Chosen Soldier: The Making of a Special Forces Warrior.* New York: Three Rivers Press, 2008,

Henderson, Charles. *Silent Warrior: The Marine Sniper's Vietnam Story Continues.* New York: Berkley, 2000.

Kyle, Chris et al. *American Sniper: The Autobiography of the Most Lethal Sniper in U.S. Military History.* New York: William Morrow, 2012.

LeBleu, Joe. *Long Rifle: A Sniper's Story in Iraq and Afghanistan.* Guilford, CTL Lyons Press, 2009.

Lunis, Natalie. *The Takedown of Osama bin Laden.* New York: Bearport, 2012.

Michaels, Jim. "U.S. Military Snipers are Changing Warfare." http://www.usatoday.com/news/military/story/2012-04-23/snipers-warfare-technology-training/54845142/1.

Montana, Jack. *Navy SEALs.* Broomall, PA: Mason Crest, 2011.

Powers, Rod. "Army Snipers School." http://usmilitary.about.com/od/armytrng/a/sniperschool.htm.

Sandler, Michael. *Army Rangers in Action.* New York: Bearport, 2008.

Bibliography
continued

Sherwood, Ben. "Lessons in Survival: The Science that Explains Why Elite Military Forces Bounce Back Faster than the Rest of Us." http://www.thedailybeast.com/newsweek/2009/02/13/lessons-in-survival.html.

Valdes, Robert. "How Military Snipers Work." http://science.howstuffworks.com/sniper.htm.

Wasdin, Howard E., and Stephen Templin. *SEAL Team Six: Memoirs of an Elite Navy SEAL Sniper*. New York: Thorndike, 2011.

Webb, Brandon. *The Red Circle: My Life in the Navy SEAL Sniper Corps and How I Trained America's Deadliest Marksmen*. New York: St. Martins, 2012.

Web sites

Army Enhanced Night Vision Goggles
http://www.army.mil/article/18980/army-fielding-enhanced-night-vision-goggles/

Army Special Forces Center
http://www.military.com/army-special-forces/training.html

Official Web site of the Navy SEALs and SWCC
http://www.sealswcc.com/

Official Web site of SEAL Team Six
http://sealteamsix.net/

Special Reconnaissance: Going Behind Enemy Lines Without Detection.
http://www.goarmy.com/special-forces/primary-missions/special-reconnaissance.html

Weapons of the Special Forces
http://www.popularmechanics.com/technology/military/1281576

Index

Photo Credits

All images used in this book that are not in the public domain are credited in the listing that follows:

Cover: Courtesy of United States Army
6-7: Courtesy of United States Army
8-9: Courtesy of United States Department of Defense
10-11: Courtesy of United States Navy
12-13: Courtesy of United States Marine Corps
15: Courtesy of United States Marine Corps
16: Courtesy of United States Department of Defense
17: Courtesy of Luhai Wong
18-19: Courtesy of United States Navy
21: Courtesy of United States Marine Corps
22-23: Courtesy of United States Army
24-25: Courtesy of United States Army
27: Courtesy of United States Government
28-29: Courtesy of United States Marine Corps
31: Courtesy of United States Department of Defense
32-33: Courtesy of United States Marine Corps
34: Courtesy of United States Marine Corps
36-37: Courtesy of United States Army
38-39: Courtesy of ISAF Headquarters Public Affairs Office
40-41: Courtesy of United States Marine Corps
44-45: Courtesy of United States Navy
46-47: Courtesy of United States Army
49: Courtesy of Library of Congress
50-51: Courtesy of United States Army
52: Courtesy of National Archives and Records Administration
53: Courtesy of United States Government
55: Courtesy of United States Marine Corps
56-57: Courtesy of United States Air Force